Math Masters

Measurement and Data

Payton's Plane Figures

Understand Concepts of Area

Oscar Luz

NEW YORK

Published in 2015 by The Rosen Publishing Group, Inc.
29 East 21st Street, New York, NY 10010

Book Design: Jonathan J. D'Rozario

Photo Credits: Cover, p. 19 (framed photographs) Syda Productions/Shutterstock.com; pp. 3, 4, 6, 8, 10, 12, 14, 16, 18, 20, 22, 23, 24 (background) VikaSuh/Shutterstock.com; p. 5 archideaphoto/Shutterstock.com; p. 7 (milk) Shah Rohani/ Shutterstock.com; p. 7 (background) Maglara/Shutterstock.com; p. 9 (cutting board) turtix/Shutterstock.com; p. 9 (background) Luis Carlos Torres/Shutterstock.com; p.11 (cheetah's face) ArtHeart/Shutterstock.com; p. 11 (book) Torian/Shutterstock.com; p. 11 (glasses) mejnak/Shutterstock.com; pp. 11, 13 (background) 3PPhoto/Shutterstock.com; p. 13 (grid paper) Ann Precious/Shutterstock.com; p. 13 (marker) jaroslava V/Shutterstock.com; p. 15 (mirror) Wayne Marques/Shutterstock.com; p. 15 (background) Ira Shumejko/Shutterstock.com; p. 17 (background) Pavel L Photo and Video/Shutterstock.com; p. 17 (game boards) reallyround/Shutterstock.com; p. 19 (background) Wth/Shutterstock.com; p. 19 (frame) hellena13/Shutterstock.com; p. 21 (TV) Tungphoto/Shutterstock.com; p. 21 (background) mmphotographie.de/ Shutterstock.com; p. 22 Johnny Adolphson/Shutterstock.com.

Library of Congress Cataloging-in-Publication Data

Luz, Oscar, author.
Payton's plane figures : understand concepts of area / Oscar Luz.
        pages cm. — (Math masters. Measurement and data)
Includes index.
ISBN 978-1-4777-4898-5 (pbk.)
ISBN 978-1-4777-4897-8 (6-pack)
ISBN 978-1-4777-6464-0 (library binding)
1. Area measurement—Juvenile literature. 2. Geometry, Plane—Juvenile literature. I. Title.
QC104.5.L89 2015
516.22—dc23
                        2014008027
Manufactured in the United States of America

CPSIA Compliance Information: Batch #WS15RC: For further information contact Rosen Publishing, New York, New York at 1-800-237-9932.

Contents

Measuring Area

Payton is learning about measuring plane figures. A plane figure is a flat shape, such as a rectangle or square. It has to be a closed shape, which is a space that's completely **enclosed** by lines.

Payton already knows how to measure perimeter. To do that, she measures the lengths of the sides of a shape and adds them together. Today, she's learning how to measure area! Perimeter and area are different. Perimeter is the length around a plane figure, while area is the amount of room inside of it.

Payton wants to go through her house and find objects that have rectangular surfaces. Then, she can measure the areas of the rectangles. How many rectangles can you find in this room?

5

In the Kitchen

Area is measured in square **units**, or the number of same-size squares that fit inside a plane figure. A unit square has 4 sides that are all 1 unit long, and it stands for 1 square unit of measurement. Payton is going to use square tiles as her unit squares to measure rectangles in her house.

First, Payton goes to her kitchen. She looks for objects that are shaped like rectangles. She finds a **carton** of milk. The side of the milk carton is a rectangle. She fills the rectangle with as many tiles as she can.

Payton lines the tiles up evenly. She makes sure there aren't any spaces between tiles and that they don't overlap. How many square units are in this rectangle? Count the unit squares to find out! This rectangle has an area of 6 square units.

6 square units

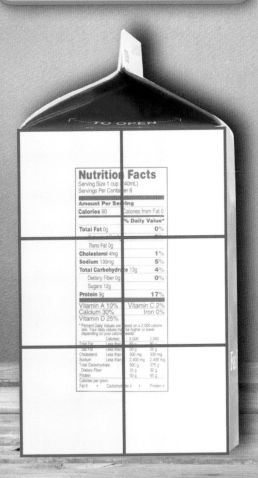

no spaces

no overlapping

Next, Payton sees a cutting board, which is also a rectangle. Her dad uses this when he cooks. He chops vegetables on the cutting board before he puts them in a salad. He also cuts fruit on the cutting board.

Payton places her square tiles on the cutting board. This rectangle is bigger than the other one. That's okay, because no matter how big or small a plane figure is, you can measure its area. Payton counts all the tiles. How many do you see?

There are 24 tiles on this rectangle. Since each tile is 1 unit square, the area of the cutting board is 24 square units.

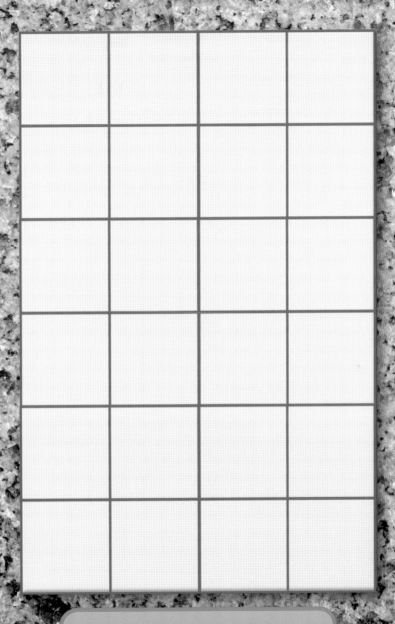

24 square units

Payton's Room

Payton goes to her bedroom next. There are lots of rectangles here! Her bed and pillows are rectangles. Her rug and desk are rectangles, too.

Payton's favorite part of her room is her bookcase. She has books about animals, art, and different hobbies. Payton picks out her favorite book from the bookcase. It's about cheetahs! She puts the tiles on the cover of the book. She makes sure none of them overlap. What else should she check before counting her tiles?

Payton should make sure there are no spaces between the tiles. Count the tiles to find the area of the book cover. There are 35 square tiles, so the book cover has an area of 35 square units.

35 square units

Reading is one of Payton's favorite hobbies, but she also loves to make art. Payton's dad bought her a desk so she can do art **projects** in her room.

Payton has colored pencils and regular pencils for drawing. She has markers and crayons for coloring. She also has paintbrushes and paint. Payton paints on **canvas**, but she usually draws on special paper. She measures the area of her paper. It's 80 square units. That's a lot of tiles to count! Payton wonders if there's a faster way to find area.

Payton learns that if she multiplies the length and width units of a rectangle, the answer shows how many square units it is made of. The length is 10 units and the width is 8 units. Since 10 times 8 is 80, the area of the paper is 80 square units.

length 10 units

width 8 units

10 units
x 8 units
____
80 square units

13

The next rectangles Payton measures are her **mirrors**. She has a big mirror and a small mirror in her room.

Payton guesses that the bigger mirror has greater area than the smaller mirror. She puts her tiles over the surface of the mirrors to check. She's right! The big mirror's area is 72 square units and the small mirror's area is 42 square units. The bigger something is, the more tiles it takes to fill it. Payton counts the tiles, but it takes a long time. Is there a faster way?

A faster way to find area is to measure the length and width, and then multiply them together. The big mirror's length is 9 units and the width is 8 units. Since 9 times 8 is 72, the area is 72 square units. The small mirror is 7 units by 6 units, so its area is 42 square units.

length 9

width 8

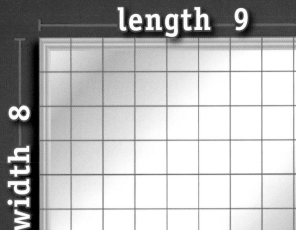

length 7

width 6

9 x 8 = 72

7 x 6 = 42

15

Payton finds more rectangles in her family room. Payton's family likes to watch movies, do **puzzles**, and play games together in this room.

Payton finds board games. She measures one board game, which looks like a long, thin rectangle. It's 10 units long and 4 units wide. She multiplies 10 and 4 to get 40, which means the area is 40 square units. She finds another game shaped like a rectangle. It's 8 units long and 5 units wide.

Since 8 times 5 is 40, the second game also has an area of 40 square units. Even though the rectangles look different and have different side lengths, they have the same area.

$$10 \times 4 = 40$$

WILD WILD WEST

$$8 \times 5 = 40$$

Payton's mom loves to take pictures of her family. She puts them in frames and hangs them on the wall in the family room.

The picture frames are different sizes, and Payton wants to measure them. She measures the first picture frame and finds that it's 12 units long and 4 units wide. Its area is 48 square units. She measures a second picture frame and finds that it's 8 units long and 6 units wide. What's the area of the second picture frame?

Both picture frames have an area of 48 square units, even though they have different side lengths. Rectangles with different perimeters sometimes have the same area.

12 x 4 = 48

8 x 6 = 48

Payton loves to watch movies with her family. Sometimes they watch cartoon movies, and other times they watch movies with real actors in them.

Payton wants to measure her family's television screen. It's very big, so Payton knows it will take many tiles to cover it. She realizes that she can measure just the sides with tiles, and then multiply the side lengths to get the area. She finds that the television is 12 units long by 7 units wide.

What's the area of the television screen?
Multiply 12 by 7 to find out!

12 x 7 = 84 square units

Backyard Area

Payton's dad says it's important to know area when you're gardening. His garden is 5 feet by 8 feet. Payton realizes that's the same as a rectangle filled with 40 squares with 1-foot sides. Now that she knows the exact measurement of the unit square, Payton knows the garden has an area of 40 square feet.

Today, Payton learned how to find area with square tiles. Can you measure the area of rectangles in your home?

5 feet
x 8 feet
———
40 square feet

Glossary

canvas (KAN-vuhs) Heavy, strong cloth that can be used for painting.

carton (KAHR-tuhn) A box made of heavy paper.

enclose (ihn-KLOHZ) To surround something completely.

mirror (MIHR-uhr) A smooth surface that shows an image of whatever is in front of it.

project (PRAH-jehkt) A task.

puzzle (PUH-zuhl) A toy with many pieces that can be put together to form a picture.

unit (YOO-nuht) A standard amount by which things are measured.

Index

Due to the changing nature of Internet links, The Rosen Publishing Group, Inc., has developed an online list of websites related to the subject of this book. This site is updated regularly. Please use this link to access the list: www.powerkidslinks.com/mm/mad/ppf